WORDS *of* H  ⌐ING

THE
ANGER
of GRIEF

How to Understand, Embrace,
and Restoratively Express
Explosive Emotions after a Loss

Alan D. Wolfelt, Ph.D.

Companion
PRESS

An imprint of the Center for Loss and Life Transition | Fort Collins, Colorado

Companion Press is an imprint of the Center for Loss and Life Transition, 3735 Broken Bow Road, Fort Collins, Colorado 80526.

27 26 25 24 23 22   6 5 4 3 2 1

ISBN: 978-1-61722-313-6

CONTENTS

WELCOME

"Anger is like flowing water; there's nothing wrong with it as long as you let it flow. Hate is like stagnant water—anger that you denied yourself the freedom to feel. Allow yourself to feel anger, allow your waters to flow... Be human."

— C. JoyBell C.

If you're reading this book, you are probably feeling angry after the death of someone loved or another significant life loss (or you're trying to help someone else who is).

The first thing I want to do is assure you that all your emotions are normal. While anger, rage, hate, blame, resentment, bitterness, and envy in grief can be unpleasant and sometimes even scary, they are normal. There's nothing wrong with you.

Yet unfortunately, there is a social stigma associated with anger. It implies that people who are angry are out of control or emotionally immature. It shames people experiencing anger.

While it's true that behaviors associated with anger can be out of control and harmful, the anger itself is a natural human emotion. Almost everyone experiences anger at some point. Your anger is often trying to teach you something about the loss as well as about yourself.

IN A CRISIS

If your anger feels so aggressive and volatile that you are at risk of harming yourself or someone else or doing damage to property, please see a counselor immediately. In a crisis, call 911. You need assistance with de-escalation and then, after that, anger management and grief companioning. You are in pain and deserve compassionate support.

The best way to overcome any stigma is to shine a light on the issue and begin to discuss it openly, honestly, and lovingly. So let's talk about your explosive emotions. Let's help you discover how to understand and embrace them. And let's identify ways for you to restoratively express them.

The goal is to help you find a path through and beyond the anger of grief. I've been a grief counselor for over four decades, and over the years a number of grievers have sought my help specifically to deal with their anger. While anger and its associated explosive emotions are normal, they can become harmful. Sustained or volatile anger stresses the body and causes illness. It can lead to depression and prevent happiness and joy. It also tends to block connection and love.

One man I met was so intensely angry over the death of his young daughter to a brain tumor that he ended up losing his marriage, a series of jobs, and ultimately his life. He refused to work to understand, calm, and heal his anger, and he ended up dying alone and still explosively angry.

Anger is something to be experienced and worked through—not lived in, day in and day out, forever. Let's get started.

MY ANGER

Before we go any further, please take a moment to jot down a few notes about anger or any explosive emotions you've been experiencing.

Since the loss, I've been feeling _____

_____

_____

_____

_____

_____

_____

I think I've been angry about the loss because _____

_____

_____

_____

_____

_____

I'm reading this book to _____

_____

_____

_____

_____

_____

_____

The Anger of Grief

THE EXPLOSIVE EMOTIONS

I call the feelings in this list collectively the "explosive emotions" because they tend to explode outside of you—sometimes in ways that are harmful to you or others. But they don't always explode—sometimes they fester inside. If you've been harboring anger without sharing it in some way, this isn't good, either. Throughout this book, I'll often use the terms "anger" and "explosive emotions" more or less interchangeably.

Anger
Rage
Hate
Blame
Resentment
Deep Frustration
Bitterness
Envy/Jealousy

It's important to understand that the explosive emotions are forms of protest. When we don't like something that's happened, especially if we think it's unfair, we naturally get mad. It's built into our biology. Children are often our best teachers about grief. Think of the toddler whose favorite toy is yanked out of their hands. This toddler wants the toy; when it's taken, their instinctive reaction is to scream or cry or hit. When someone loved is taken from you or you experience another significant life loss, your instinctive reaction may be much the same.

Relatedly, the explosive emotions are rooted in the concept of fairness. Whenever we believe that something "should be" a certain way, we often feel angry if it doesn't turn out that way. Again, our anger is in protest to what we perceive as an injustice. It's an emotion based on our expectations and understanding of social norms. If a child dies of cancer, for example, we feel that the death is unfair. Young people should not die. We might rage over this injustice. Smoldering anger—also called bitterness—may set in.

What's more, blame, resentment, and envy are natural outgrowths of our feelings of injustice. When something unfair happens, we tend to look for someone or something to blame. We might resent others whose outcomes in a similar situation were better. And we might be envious of those who seem to live a charmed life untouched by injustice or loss.

ENVY OR JEALOUSY?

Envy is when we feel the lack of something we don't have that others do. Jealousy is when we feel threatened that something we have might be taken away from us. In grief, envy is common. If your young adult son dies and you attend the wedding of one of

The Anger of Grief

his friends, you might naturally experience envy. If your husband is terminally ill and others consume the bulk of his waning energy, you might feel jealousy. We often use these terms interchangeably. In grief, you might experience one, both, or neither.

And here we arrive at an essential truth about the explosive emotions: they tend to feel active and powerful. When we're angry, we're riled up. We've got righteousness in our corner, and we're fixing for a fight. And if we act out in anger, we may feel like we're at least "doing something." Anger can bolster our feelings of agency and self-esteem.

Relatedly, anger may give us a false sense of control over things that are not in our control. It's often (but not always) outward-directed. It focuses on other people and situations, and it tries to tell them what they should have done, what they should do, and how they should be. This is part of the power construct of anger.

In the face of great loss, the sense of forceful energy we get from the explosive emotions often feels better than our more passive, vulnerable, inward feelings of sadness, helplessness, guilt, fear, and anxiety. Yet as we'll see, it can also be human nature to nurture the explosive emotions for too long in an attempt (conscious or unconscious) to deny, mask, or indefinitely defer our deeper, more passive pain. This path, however, leads to unhealed grief and a severely diminished life.

GRIEF, MOURNING, AND EXPLOSIVE EMOTIONS

Grief is everything you think and feel inside of you after a loss. It's all your thoughts and emotions, which change from day to day. Grief is normal and natural.

Mourning is when you express those thoughts and feelings outside of yourself. Talking about your loss experience is mourning. So are crying, journaling, sharing online, attending a support group, and seeing a counselor. Essentially, your behaviors related to your grief are your mourning.

The explosive emotions you feel inside you are part of your grief. But they're not all of your grief. You probably feel other emotions about the loss, as well, such as sadness and fear.

When you express your explosive emotions, you're mourning. Mourning is a good thing because it's how you move toward healing. Mourning is what makes all your grief feelings soften. It gives your grief momentum and helps you integrate your loss experience into your ongoing life.

The Anger of Grief

HEALING IN GRIEF

To heal in grief means to become whole again, to integrate your grief into your self and to find a path to continue your changed life with fullness and meaning. Your explosive emotions are part of your grief, and to heal them you will learn to understand them, befriend them, and express them in restorative ways. Through this process your explosive emotions will soften, allowing you to move through and beyond the intensity with which you are experiencing them now.

THE PHYSIOLOGY OF EXPLOSIVE EMOTIONS

Stop reading for a moment and see if you can conjure the explosive emotion that's been strongest for you lately. Search for it inside you, and stir it up with your thoughts. What does it feel like in your body? Where do you feel it? What are the qualities of the feeling? If you were to describe the bodily sensation to a friend, what would you say?

Anger feels hot, right? It's agitating. It burns and is associated with fire. Some of the sayings we've developed about anger give us insight into its effects on our bodies and social interactions:

- *He went ballistic.*
- *She's up in arms.*
- *My blood boiled.*

- *Don't blow your top!*
- *He bit my head off.*
- *I was seeing red.*

Anger feels hot because it arouses our sympathetic nervous system, which controls the body's involuntary responses. It elevates our heart rate, blood pressure, and breathing rate, and it drenches us in stress chemicals like adrenaline and cortisol. Scientists believe that anger, like fear, was an evolutionary necessity. It gave us the focus and the burst of energy we needed when our lives were in peril. You've probably heard of the body's "fight, flight, or freeze" response to danger. Anger is the "fight" part of this equation.

But the anger you're feeling in your grief isn't caused by an immediate physical threat—it's caused by an emotional and spiritual injury to your heart. The trouble is, our bodies and the primitive parts of our brains haven't developed good mechanisms for differentiating the two. Our bodies react in the same way whether we're in actual peril or we're experiencing a psychological hazard.

UNDERSTANDING YOUR ANGER

"If you get angry easily, it may be because the seed of anger in you has been watered frequently over many years."

— Nhat Hanh

Your anger makes sense. It arises for reasons that are understandable. Becoming acquainted with your anger in particular as well as anger in general will help you embrace and heal it.

THE UTILITY OF ANGER

Anger exists. Accepting it as a normal human emotion is the first step toward integrating it into your life story.

But anger is also functional. As a "fight" response to an immediate threat, anger's evolutionary purpose is to spur us to respond aggressively when we need to, in order to save our life or the lives of those we love. In the modern world, we rarely have to fight for our lives, but still, anger can move us to take necessary action. If we use anger to motivate us toward effective problem solving, for example, we're putting the evolutionary utility of anger to good use.

What's more—and this is also really important to understand—in grief, anger is a bit like the numbness and denial we naturally experience right after a loss. In the early days, numbness and denial protect us from the full force of what happened, allowing us to absorb the reality bit by bit. In fact, I often call them the shock absorbers of grief. They help us survive. Thank goodness for shock and denial! Similarly, after a loss our anger often protects us from our more helpless, painful feelings, like fear, guilt, and sadness. In fact, I often call the explosive emotions "survival-oriented protest."

So we can honor and thank our anger—for a time. Just as we must work to soften our numbness and denial in grief, we must also work to soften our anger, so that we can fully encounter the necessary pain it has done such a good job of guarding us against.

THE DANGERS OF ANGER

We talked a bit about the physiology of anger. Now I want to discuss the dangers of that physiology as well as the potential harms of long-term or volatile anger to your emotional, social, and spiritual health.

Physical

It's important to understand that while anger can feel

powerful, active, and even good, it's not meant to be an emotion that your body sustains for a long period of time. Evolutionarily, it's meant to give you a quick burst of energy. When anger is prolonged, on the other hand, it stresses the body. Studies have shown strong correlations between anger and high blood pressure, stroke, heart disease, and a weakened immune system. Anger makes people sick, and it even kills them.

Emotional

Scientists have found that anger is linked to anxiety and depression. Again, anger is a normal human emotion, but feeling angry all the time is not normal. A tendency toward volatile, angry outbursts is also physically, emotionally, and socially damaging.

Social

You may well have already discovered that your anger can be off-putting to others. Because anger is often blameful, aggressive, and even violent, it tends to harm relationships and can traumatize others in its path. It's hard to be around someone who's angry all the time. And it's scary to be around someone who's volatile, who may explode at the slightest trigger at any moment. In these ways, pronounced anger can throw up significant roadblocks to love and connection.

Spiritual

Spiritual health requires devoting time regularly to searching for and connecting with those things that feel most meaningful to you in your short stay here on earth (and, depending on your beliefs, beyond that). To a large degree, wrestling with anger is about wrestling with the big "whys" of human existence. Why do bad things happen? Why are we here? In this way, anger and spirituality may naturally go hand-in-hand. But ongoing, unrelenting anger can also get in the way of spiritual experiences like awe, gratitude, and joy.

THE WOLFELT ANGER INVENTORY

Let's take a minute to learn more about your particular experiences with anger, both in relation to your recent loss and more generally, to see how explosive emotions are part of your life story and personality.

I've created the following questionnaire to help you take a closer look at your anger and begin to identify areas of focus for restoratively expressing and reconciling it. Next to each statement, please circle the number that fits best. As you read each question, please consider not only anger but all the explosive emotions.

THE WOLFELT ANGER INVENTORY Next to each statement, circle the number that fits best.	Never	Rarely	Sometimes	Often
In the household I grew up in, people seemed noticeably angry, whether inwardly or outwardly.	1	2	3	4
As a child and young person, I believe I felt anger or other explosive emotions more than my friends and peers.	1	2	3	4
As a child and young person, the adults in my life modeled unhealthy expressions of anger.	1	2	3	4
FAMILY OF ORIGIN SCORE (out of 12)				
In the past, there have been times I have felt angry about a life loss but didn't express that anger.	1	2	3	4
I still feel unreconciled anger about things that happened earlier in my life.	1	2	3	4
Anger has been a prominent part of my life.	1	2	3	4
CARRIED GRIEF SCORE (out of 12)				
I feel generalized anger and can't always identify why.	1	2	3	4
I feel anger about this loss.	1	2	3	4

Continued on next page...

	1	2	3	4
I feel angry but do not express my anger.	1	2	3	4
When I'm angry lately, I tend to withdraw and isolate.	1	2	3	4
I'm afraid of what my anger might be protecting me from.	1	2	3	4
INTERNAL ANGER SCORE (out of 20)				
I blow up at strangers or casual acquaintances.	1	2	3	4
Others tell me I'm an angry person.	1	2	3	4
I hurt other people with my anger.	1	2	3	4
People I care about are afraid of my temper.	1	2	3	4
My expressions of anger make me uncomfortable, embarrassed, or scared.	1	2	3	4
EXTERNAL ANGER SCORE (out of 20)				
I wish I didn't feel so angry.	1	2	3	4
I need to better acknowledge and understand my anger.	1	2	3	4
I need to develop healthier ways of expressing my anger.	1	2	3	4
My anger is blocking healing, peace, love, and joy.	1	2	3	4
ANGER AWARENESS SCORE (out of 16)				
TOTAL SCORE (out of 80)				

Before we talk about anger scores, I want to emphasize that anger is not truly a measurable experience. The scale I've created is meant only to help you begin to understand your anger better. With that caveat firmly in mind, I invite you to use this rubric to get a sense of the extent of your anger issues.

0-25	Minimal anger
26-40	Mild anger
41-60	Moderate anger
61-80	Severe anger

In addition to helping you understand the severity of your anger, the labeled sections in the chart will also give you some hints about where to concentrate your energies as you work on reconciling your anger. If your internal anger score is high but your external anger score is low, for example, you may simply be expressing your anger in healthy ways or you may not be expressing your anger nearly enough. If your carried grief and family of origin scores are high, you may need the support of a counselor in understanding how your early experiences with anger and loss are shaping your current struggles—and what to do about that. And since awareness is the first step toward positive change, your anger awareness score measures how conscious you are of any pronounced anger issues and your readiness to work on them.

CONTRIBUTORS TO ANGER IN GRIEF

Here are some common contributors to anger in grief. As you read through them, put a checkmark next to any that might apply to you.

☐ *Circumstances of the loss*

Understandably, this is often a major contributor to anger after a loss. Remember that feelings about fairness and justice are often at the heart of explosive emotions. Do you feel something about the loss was unfair? Was it premature? Was it caused by someone else? Did it happen to someone it shouldn't have?

Homicides, suicides, accidental deaths, and deaths caused by acts of nature are among the types of losses that we tend to feel are violations of the ways things are supposed to happen. Violent deaths, in particular, may stir our "fight" response and can arouse our own feelings of aggression and retribution.

Significant losses other than the death of a loved one can also provoke anger, of course. Serious illness or injury, for example, often feels deeply unfair. Job or financial losses can naturally spark explosive emotions. Betrayal, separation, and divorce are other loss types that commonly generate lingering anger.

In addition, circumstances that keep us from acknowledging a loss, embracing our feelings, and supporting one another via traditional rituals can inflame our frustration and anger. If you weren't able to gather for a funeral, for example, you may not have had an opportunity to express your feelings in the company of others who understand. Social isolation and lack of communication can compound anger.

IS YOUR ANGER JUSTIFIED?

When a loss is caused by the harmful act of others—intentional or unintentional—we tend to sanction the resulting anger of grief. The more unjust the cause of the loss, the more understandable the anger. Homicide is a clear example of this. If someone you love is killed by another person, society deems your fury legitimate.

In such cases, of course anger is to be expected! If you've experienced a flagrantly unforgivable loss, your anger is indeed justified. But what I want you to keep in mind as you read this book is that all feelings in all grief situations are legitimate. Over my many decades as a grief counselor, I've found that it's unhelpful to compare losses and grief responses. Grief is complicated and arises not only from a specific incident but from an entire lifetime of experiences. Who "gets" to be angry and who doesn't in the aftermath of a loss is not a valid distinction. The truth is that anyone who is angry gets to be angry.

If your explosive emotions in grief stem from a readily understandable cause, you will likely experience more empathy and support from the people around you. If your anger seems "unjustified," on the other hand—to yourself or to others—you may struggle more with learning to understand it, express it, and receive support for it. Either way, though, your anger is real, valid, and deserving of attention, expression, and compassion.

☐ *Your relationship with the person who is the object of your anger*
Unexpected deaths often result in feelings of unfinished business. Regardless of who is "at fault," you may be angry at the person who died and/or at yourself over longstanding or unreconciled relationship issues. It's beyond frustrating to be forever robbed of the opportunity to clear the air and make things right.

If your anger is directed at people who are still alive, the unique features of your relationships and history with them will also affect your anger.

☐ *Family-of-origin experience*
When you were growing up, how was anger modeled in your home? When your parents were angry, did they yell at each other or at you? Did they throw or break things? Did they assault each other or you? What about the other adult caregivers in your life? And when you were mad and upset, how was your anger responded to?

We learn so much about how to "be" from our parents and other adult caregivers. You may have been taught that it's normal to be volatile and perhaps even violent. Or maybe you learned that anger and other strong emotions are shameful; if you're angry, you should keep it stuffed inside. Or possibly you were shown how anger, deep love, and mutual respect can coexist.

Your anger style was affected by your upbringing. You may be repeating patterns you learned at home, or you may have chosen, consciously or unconsciously, to do the opposite. Whatever your go-to anger script is, it is probably now coming to the fore in your grief. What was your "Family of Origin Score" on page 15? A high score indicates that you may have deep-seated anger habits to learn more about.

☐ *Personality factors*

Some of us are introverts, and some are extroverts. Some are risk-takers, and others are cautious. Some engage with their hearts, and some lead with their minds. Some are doers, and some are observers. Independent of your upbringing at home, you have grown into a unique individual shaped by all kinds of people, life experiences, cultural influences, and genetics. Your anger response in grief will be influenced by all of it.

In addition, your self-esteem plays a role in your anger response. When faced with a major loss, people with a strong sense of authority and power in their own lives may more naturally direct their explosive emotions at others as a means of coping. After all, they may realize, assertiveness has seen them through many challenges in their lives. People with more vulnerable self-esteem, on the other hand, might react to loss with self-directed anger and/or unexpressed anger at others.

☐ Carried grief

Obviously, life is a series of losses and transitions. It is likely that your life experiences so far have included significant losses other than the loss that is arousing your anger right now. If so, you may be carrying old grief that is contributing to your current explosive emotions. Unreconciled issues from our past often affect our ongoing lives in ways we don't fully appreciate or understand.

Over the years, anger can really snowball. Take a look at your "Carried Grief Score" on page 15. If it's 9 or higher, you may essentially be rolling old anger into your current anger without realizing it.

For more on carried grief, you may want to see my book *Living in the Shadow of the Ghosts of Grief*.

☐ Your current life circumstances and relationships

How was your life going before this recent loss? If you were already struggling—with relationships, family, career, health, finances, or other major stressors—the loss may feel like the straw that broke the camel's back. Alternately, your life may have been going along just fine, but you now realize you lack the intimate relationships you need for adequate emotional and social support.

☐ *Your spirituality*

Do religious and spiritual background and beliefs influence anger? Absolutely! Maybe you were taught that God is vengeful and punishment is just. Or maybe you learned that God is loving and forgiving, and you should be, too. Or perhaps you came to understand that anger is an expression of the ego, not the soul. As you get to know your anger, consider how your spiritual beliefs may be part of the mix.

These aren't all the contributors to anger in grief, of course, but they're the ones I've seen most in my forty years counseling people in grief. As you read this section, did you think of other influences on your explosive emotions since the loss? Write them down below.

Possible contributors to my explosive emotions in grief:

_____

_____

_____

_____

THE NEEDS OF MOURNING

Your anger is a symptom of your grief. To reconcile your grief requires expressing it outside of yourself, or mourning it. In your journey through mourning, you must meet six needs along the way to healing.

THE SIX NEEDS OF MOURNING

1. Acknowledge the reality of the loss

2. Embrace the pain

3. Remember the person or attachment

4. Develop a new self-identity

5. Search for meaning

6. Let others help you—now and always

While a full discussion of the six needs of mourning is beyond the scope of this resource, here I want to highlight a couple of the needs that have particular relevance to anger. (For more on the six needs, please see my book *Understanding Your Grief*.)

The first need of mourning is to acknowledge the reality of the loss. Remember how we've emphasized that anger is a protest emotion? Like denial, anger and the other explosive emotions are ways your mind tries to protect you from fully acknowledging a painful reality. So in addition to getting to know and expressing your anger itself, the most essential way to work on softening your anger is to work on acknowledging the reality of the loss.

Anything that helps you understand and come to terms with the facts of the loss is a step in the right direction. If you have lingering questions or potentially inaccurate assumptions about what happened, learn more. Muster the courage to ask questions, talk to others with additional information, gather many perspectives, and flesh out the story. Don't look away—look towards. I know this process can be extremely painful, but I assure you it will help you acknowledge the reality and thus gain momentum in moving through your anger.

More broadly, telling the story of the loss will help you more deeply acknowledge its reality, so that you come to understand it not only with your head, but with your heart. Talk about the loss. Tell others what happened. Include all the elements of the timeline of the story: the prologue, the beginning, the middle, the climax, the ending, and the epilogue.

Doing memory work—the third need of mourning—will also help you acknowledge the reality of the loss and thus soften your anger. Spend time looking at old photos and memorabilia. Put together a box of special snapshots and keepsakes. Share memories with others. Write down memories in a journal. The more you purposefully remember the "before" as well as the time of the loss itself, the more the reality will become integrated into your life. Memory work also helps grievers make the important transition from focusing on the loss to focusing on gratitude for the good times.

OWNING YOUR ANGER

Sometimes people with a tendency toward anger blame others—or life—for their explosive emotions. "I'm only angry because you're doing something that makes me angry!" they say. Or, "I'm angry because this wrong or frustrating thing keeps happening to me!"

Yet as you begin to better understand your anger, you may also begin to realize that living in anger is a choice. Your anger is not someone else's fault—it is your response to an external reality. It may well be a natural and understandable response, but nonetheless, it is one you can choose or not choose, day by day, moment by moment.

To own your anger means to accept responsibility for it. I'm not saying you should be ashamed of it. I'm suggesting you should claim it. I'm saying you should be aware of it, acknowledge it, and consciously decide what to do with it.

The more you befriend your anger, the more you'll learn why it's such a prominent part of your unique grief experience—and what may lie beneath it.

Think of your anger like a protective sibling or friend. When you're in a bad situation, your friend may come to your rescue and stand between you and whatever's threatening you. They may even get aggressive in an attempt to save you from being hurt.

It's probable that your anger is similarly shielding you. If your anger weren't there to rage and bluster and protect you, what thoughts and feelings might be hurting you, instead? Feeling this through is part of your journey through anger.

Helplessness in the aftermath of a major loss can be really painful. So instead of acknowledging our thoughts and feelings of helplessness, we might get angry. We've talked about how anger is action-oriented and gives us a sense of control. We're not helpless—we're furious! But as we work through our explosive emotions, we often find that as part of the healing process, we must reconcile ourselves to our lack of control in life. We are, in fact, helpless in the face of many normal losses, and coming to terms with this reality is often a long, difficult journey.

Relatedly, **fear** is a common emotion that anger guards

against. After a big loss, it's perfectly natural to feel afraid. Life can be so scary and overwhelming! How will you cope with your new reality? How will you go on? Will someone else you care about get sick or die, or will another major loss occur soon? What about finances and other practical matters? How will you possibly manage? As C.S. Lewis famously wrote, "No one ever told me that grief felt so much like fear."

When we are fearful, anxious, or worry-filled, we feel vulnerable. Fear makes us want to hide or run away. It's the "freeze" and "flight" parts of the fight, flight, or freeze response to danger. When powerful, action-oriented anger steps aside, we often find the normal fears of grief cowering behind it.

Regret and guilt often underlie anger as well. People in grief commonly experience regret and guilt because of the finality of death and other types of losses. We naturally wonder if we could have done things differently. We agonize over mistakes made and opportunities missed. Yet for all our normal "what ifs" and regrets, it's too late to make amends or undo past decisions.

Guilt and regret focus on the past, and anger lives in the present. It's hard but necessary grief work to come to terms with any guilt and regret we may be harboring, and anger—

though it's trying to protect us—tends to keep us from that work.

Sadness and loss are the other main emotions that anger sometimes protects us from. In fact, I believe sadness to be the most challenging emotion to acknowledge, embrace, and reconcile in grief. Sadness naturally makes us feel bad. It saps all the color and pleasure from our lives. It makes it hard to get out of bed in the morning, and it can even cause us to question if we want to continue living.

Like helplessness, fear, and guilt, sadness and loss are also vulnerable, passive emotions. And they're particularly painful. Anger doesn't want us to feel them, so it often protects us from them. But if we are to reconcile our grief, we must also acknowledge and embrace our sadness. We can't do that if anger keeps sheltering us from it.

LIFE ISN'T FAIR

From the time we're born, we naturally become attached to people, pets, places, things, and situations. These loves of our life are our greatest joy and privilege. The trouble is, circumstances constantly change. People get sick. People age. People die. Pets too. People make mistakes. People betray us. We betray ourselves. Passions ebb and flow. Fortunes rise and fall. And many of these changes feel deeply unfair. But no matter what happens, the world just keeps turning.

When things go wrong—or change in ways we don't like—we call these turns of event "losses." And as we've said, it's natural to protest loss. It's normal to get angry. The longer we live, though, the more the losses pile up. We learn that loss and change are unavoidable. We learn that no matter how angry we get, we can't control what happens. And if we're lucky, we begin to understand that living in anger over these losses—even the unfair ones—has a shadow effect. Anger blocks the light of vulnerability, connection, joy, and love. Sustained, hardened anger can cause us to die while we're still alive.

Whatever you are angry about, it was probably unfair, and I am truly sorry. I'm also hopeful that the principles in this little book will help you find your way through and beyond your anger so that you can live and love fully again.

THE "WHY" EXERCISE

To better understand the emotions that may lie beneath your anger, consider digging deeper and deeper as you ask yourself "why" questions. Here's an example:

- How do I feel? *Angry.*

- Why am I angry?
  Because this death should not have happened.

- Why should this death not have happened?
  Because a driver made a stupid mistake!

- Why did a driver make a mistake?
  Because he was looking at his phone.

- Why was he looking at this phone?
  Because he thought he could do two things at once, which is a terrible mistake.

- Why did he make a mistake?
  Because he was careless. Also because everyone makes mistakes. It's part of being human.

- Why are mistakes part of being human?
  Because it's just how it is! People aren't perfect. Nobody's perfect. I'm not perfect. I've made mistakes, too.

- How do I feel about the reality that people are imperfect?
  Angry. Frustrated. Helpless. Sad.

Do you see how continuing to ask why questions can get you through and beneath the anger of a protest thought or feeling about the loss? In this case, the why questions bring us down to the understanding that while mistakes hurt people, they're also normal and, broadly speaking, unavoidable. This bottom-line reality makes us feel helpless and sad.

Of course, I'm not suggesting that the why exercise will instantly reconcile your anger. Nothing will do that. But if you repeat the exercise over time, it may help you get to know your anger better as well as the more vulnerable emotions in its shadows.

COMPLICATED GRIEF AND ANGER

Ongoing, unrelenting anger (or another explosive emotion) is often a symptom of what therapists term "complicated grief." Complicated grief isn't a disorder or illness; it's simply normal grief that has gotten stuck or off-track somehow, usually due to complicated loss circumstances.

I call grief that's stuck on a strong feeling such as anger "impasse grief" because the anger is creating an impasse to healing. It's like a giant boulder blocking a narrow mountain trail. You can't go around it. You can't go under it. You can't get over it. So every day you rage at the rock, and you go nowhere.

Is your anger the main or most pronounced feeling in your grief, even if seems like you're often mad at things other than the loss itself? Have you been feeling your anger strongly for many months or years now—without it diminishing (and maybe even with it growing) over time? If you've answered yes to these questions, you're probably experiencing complicated grief. I hope this book will help you understand, embrace, and express your anger so that it begins to soften. I also encourage you to make an appointment with a compassionate counselor. Seeing an experienced grief counselor for a period of weeks or months may be just the extra help you need to roll the boulder aside and find a way through this impasse to hope and healing.

EMBRACING YOUR ANGER

"Ultimately, healthy grief requires that explosive emotions,
when present, be expressed, not repressed."

— Dr. Alan D. Wolfelt

No matter the reasons for your anger in grief, it's essential to acknowledge and befriend it.

While this may seem counterintuitive, your anger is not your enemy—it's your friend. It's there to teach you. Once you find ways to embrace your anger and learn the lessons it offers, it will naturally begin to soften.

SITTING WITH YOUR ANGER

Perhaps the first step to embracing the anger of your grief is learning to sit with it. The next time you feel anger or another explosive emotion, don't say anything or take any action. Instead, find a quiet spot and simply sit with it.

Let it wash over you. Notice what it feels like in your body. Pay attention to the thoughts coursing through your mind. In other words, observe your inner thoughts and feelings with kindness and compassion.

While you're doing so, breathe slowly and deeply. Breathe in to a count of five and out to a count of five. Breathe from your diaphragm. Consciously relax all your muscles, which are probably tensed because of the fight response. If you feel the need to release some energy, walk instead of sitting.

Mindfully experiencing your anger in this way will help you begin to develop a new relationship with it. You will begin to realize that:

1. Anger is a feeling in the body.
2. Angry thoughts come and go.
3. Anger does not require aggressive expression in order to dissipate.
4. You can calm yourself, often in just a few minutes.

THE FIVE-MINUTE RESET

When you feel angry:

1. Stop what you're doing.
2. Breathe deeply.
3. Close your eyes. Feel your anger in your body, and notice your thoughts.
4. After a couple of minutes, open your eyes. Turn your attention from your anger to your surroundings. Observe the sights,

sounds, textures, and smells around you. Keep breathing deeply.

5. Now that you're calmer, ask yourself: Why was I feeling angry? Is there anything I can learn from this encounter with anger?

SOOTHING YOUR ANGER

In the heat of the moment, anger can be soothed by sitting with it and actively but quietly attending to it. When you honor the anger of your grief by giving it the mindful attention it deserves, it will dissolve. It may even begin to open the door and allow you to start to get acquainted with the more passive, painful emotions it may be masking.

Here are some other ways to soothe your anger:

• *Talk to a friend or loved one.*
Expressing your grief out loud in a nonaggressive conversation will not only release the explosive energy, it will also allow you to tell the story of your anger. The more you tell the story, the less overpowering it will become. Talking tames anger.

• *Write in a journal.*
Expressing yourself in writing, whether in a paper journal or on your computer or another device, is another way of allowing yourself to mourn. This can be an excellent tool for self-understanding and reconciliation. In writing, you

don't need to worry about being aggressive or traumatizing a listener. You can say whatever you want with as much venom as you want.

• *Write a letter.*
Similarly, writing a letter—perhaps to the object of your anger—will help you give voice to your explosive thoughts and feelings. Who or what are you angry with? Write them a letter detailing everything that's inside you. Be completely honest. Say everything you haven't been able to say out loud. When the letter is finished, however, don't send it. Put it somewhere safe, and get it out again a month from now. Reread it. Consider sharing it with a friend—someone you know to be a good empathizer and who is equipped to hear your anger story.

• *Try yoga and/or meditation.*
Learning to work with your breath and inhabit your body while letting your thoughts flow past you is an excellent way to allow your anger to be without getting caught up in it.

• *Exercise.*
Physical activity isn't good only for the body—it's good for the mind and soul. You're learning that your anger lives in your body and your mind. When you exercise your body, you change its biochemistry. You dispel the stress chemicals

of anger, and you flood the nervous system instead with feel-good chemicals like dopamine and oxytocin. Exercise also pumps more oxygen into the brain, stimulates neural connections, and fuels optimism.

• *Pamper yourself.*
When you're angry, your body is tense and under stress. Activities that pamper the body will naturally help release the anger. Try soaking in a bath or getting a massage. Take a nap. Get a manicure and pedicure. Treat yourself to a favorite food or beverage. Use aromatherapy. Wrap yourself in a cozy blanket or sweater.

When it comes to soothing anger, the trick is to find techniques that work for you. So keep trying until you've put together an anger toolkit—your go-to strategies to calm yourself whenever the need arises. The goal is to allow yourself to feel your anger, in doses, without it consuming your entire day and life. Your anger belongs, but it's extremely unhealthy to live in anger.

WHAT IF YOU'RE ANGRY AT YOURSELF?

Self-directed anger is somewhat common in grief. Is your self-esteem low? Do you berate yourself for your behavior, body, skills, cognitive capacity, or anything else? Do you find yourself impatient or disgusted with your own self-perceived shortcomings? Do you engage in any compulsive behaviors (gambling, drug or alcohol use, shopping, etc.) in an effort to distract yourself from your own self-loathing?

On page 28, we talked about the fact that anger can mask guilt and regret, among other painful emotions. If you've been especially angry at yourself since the loss, you may actually feel deeply guilty or regretful. What's more, self-esteem issues are often rooted in childhood experiences and probably predate the loss event.

For you, the journey through and beyond anger will require working on self-compassion. No matter what, you are a precious, worthy person. A good counselor will be able to help you unearth the causes of your self-directed anger and work on mourning them as well as reclaiming your right to wholeness and love.

The Anger of Grief

RESTORATIVELY EXPRESSING YOUR ANGER

"How much more grievous are the consequences of anger than the causes of it."

— Marcus Aurelius

Soothing your anger is a way to soften it inside of you. Expressing our anger outwardly is another way to soften it. Both are necessary, important mourning tools. In this section we'll talk about the healthy expression of anger.

DAMAGING EXPRESSION VS. RESTORATIVE EXPRESSION

To move toward reconciling your grief, you absolutely need to express your explosive emotions. There is no healing without mourning. But as you explore ways to befriend and express your anger, I want you to keep in mind the difference between damaging expression and restorative expression.

Damaging expression of explosive emotions harms you or others. It hurts feelings, injures relationships, and/ or causes physical harm to something or someone. It can cause secondary trauma to others who may not be trained or equipped to make space for and process the traumatic experiences and explosive emotions of others.

Restorative expression of explosive emotions, on the other hand, allows you to fully share feelings in ways and places that are safe, nonviolent, and non-traumatizing to others. It restores your sense of equilibrium, at least temporarily, and over time can strengthen relationships and restore inner peace.

You may find this chart a handy guide.

Potentially Damaging Expression	Restorative Expression
Yelling or shouting at someone you care about.	Never yelling *at* someone else. Yelling only in the presence of an adult who has given you permission to explode and is equipped and prepared to listen without advice-giving or judgment.
Angrily blaming or intimidating others in their presence.	Expressing blameful anger in a journal or to someone other than the object of the blame and again, with permission. If a relationship requires an apology

	from a wrongdoer and/or healthy boundaries established, this is done as calmly as possible and with "I" statements.
Being passive-aggressive with your anger; sulking, withdrawing, being silent, denying, procrastinating, using sarcasm, gaslighting.	Being open and genuine about your feelings as calmly as possible and with "I" statements.
Causing physical harm to another person.	If you feel this impulse, seeing a counselor instead.
Causing physical harm to yourself or engaging in reckless behavior that may cause you physical harm.	If you feel this impulse, seeing a counselor instead. If it's an emergency, calling 911.
Causing physical harm to objects injudiciously. Being physically violent. Throwing or breaking things. Damaging property.	Using your body to express anger with intention. Using healthy, vigorous physical activities such as martial arts, running, bicycling, tennis, boxing, etc.
Expressing hate or rage online or in written communications or voicemail.	Expressing hate or rage through journaling and sharing this writing with someone prepared and equipped to read about your thoughts and feelings.

Restoratively Expressing Your Anger

	Discussing with this person the appropriateness of sharing your hate or rage directly with those you blame.
In general, reacting impulsively, without thought or intention.	In general, responding with care and intention.
Focusing on condemnation.	Focusing on conversation.

USING "I" STATEMENTS

As you learn to restoratively express your explosive emotions, "I" statements are an essential part of your anger toolkit. An "I" statement is a way of owning your thoughts and feelings and expressing them without blaming, shaming, or traumatizing the person you are talking to.

Try starting a sentence with "I feel…" For example, "I feel angry and alone" or "I feel so angry that he abandoned me."

Avoid blaming the listener. Don't say, "I feel so angry and alone because you're not there for me." Also avoid traumatizing the listener. Don't yell or share details about traumatizing events, circumstances, or rage fantasies unless the adult listener has given permission in advance and you know them to be equipped to handle it.

It's also always appropriate to ask for help. Simply saying, "I feel so angry, and I need help" instantly makes space for empathy, support, and love.

SETTING YOUR INTENTION

When possible, consider the outcomes you desire from any expressions of anger you might be considering or that you know will probably arise. Do you just want to blow off steam? Are you hoping to solve a problem? Do you want to clear something up? Are you after retribution or vengeance? How do you want those on the receiving end of your anger to feel, and why?

In advance, on paper or in your mind, fill in these blanks:

When I have the opportunity to express my anger about

_____ to _____ or in this

situation—_____— my intention is to

_____ and to leave the interaction

with everyone feeling _____

because_____.

As you envision the scene, imagine yourself—your body language, your tone, your facial expressions, the words you'll use—as well as the reactions of the other people present.

Setting your intention is a way of mentally rehearsing anger behaviors and goals. It will help you be mindful and restorative in your expressions.

ON LASHING OUT

So is it ever appropriate to lash out angrily at someone?

First, I think angry outbursts are a normal human response. We're not perfect. We can't always help it. We can't always mindfully control our explosive emotions, and we sometimes do or say harmful things and need to apologize in the aftermath.

But at the same time, anger eruptions are rarely constructive or restorative. They may feel powerful and justified in the moment, but they often become traumatic memories in the long run. They can never be taken back. If you say something deeply hurtful to someone you care about, they won't forget it. Trust can erode, and intimacy may be sacrificed. If, on the other hand, a person on the receiving end of an angry outburst feels they've done something wrong—something commensurate with the harshness of your expression—they may be more accepting of your condemnation.

Still, except in rare circumstances (here I think of understandable anger in response to intentional or negligent harm caused by another, such as criminal damage, injury, or death), conversation, not condemnation, is almost always a better path to problem solving and healing both for you and for the person you're angry at.

If you express outrage to someone with whom you don't have a relationship that's important to you—such as the representative of a business, an occasional colleague, a stranger on the internet, a distant family member, or a neighbor—you may feel it's OK if you explode. But again, hostility directed *at* someone else tends to slam a door. It communicates your anger, yes, but it doesn't allow for true communication or problem solving. You may well be unfairly blaming and traumatizing someone who has no control over the situation. Or it might be that you're unfairly projecting your anger about the loss onto a completely unrelated situation.

If you're prone to angry outbursts, I encourage you to work with a counselor on anger-management skills. Again, your anger is not wrong or bad, but your rage is probably hurting other people as well as yourself. A counselor can help you better understand the causes of your anger as well as develop an anger toolkit for defusing explosive emotions in the moment and expressing anger restoratively instead.

THE POWER OF THE PAUSE

When you're really angry and feeling the stress chemicals adrenaline and cortisol coursing through your body, step away and count to ten. Unless someone's in immediate danger, it's rarely a good idea to respond immediately. Calm yourself first. This will give you the brief pause you need to collect your thoughts, set your intention, and respond restoratively.

Buddhists sometimes call this the "Sacred Pause," because it helps you reach down to the feelings beneath the anger, acknowledge them with empathy and curiosity, and then respond with heightened consciousness.

MAKING RESTORATIVE EXPRESSION A HABIT

Did you find any of your anger-expression habits in the "potentially damaging" column in the chart on pages 40-42? If so, you're not alone. I would venture to say that's true for most of us.

Very few of us were taught restorative-anger expression in our formative years and beyond. Please do not feel bad or ashamed if your anger toolkit needs development. Instead, I hope you will look on this as an opportunity to grow. As Maya Angelou said, "When I knew better, I did better."

Restorative expression of anger is a skill. And like any skill, you get better at it with intention and practice.

One way to do this is by working with a counselor. A trained, experienced grief counselor will be able to help you with your grief in general and your explosive emotions in particular. If your anger score on page 17 falls into the moderate or severe range, I'd suggest seeing a counselor for a few sessions to see if it helps you get started on understanding and processing your anger.

Another way to build the restorative-expression habit is by working with a responsibility partner. Is there someone you know who's also working on some aspect of personal growth (it could be anger; it could be something else)? If so, maybe you could partner with that person for mutual discussion, support, and accountability. Meeting with another person regularly to talk about your challenges and successes is a wonderful way to build a relationship as well as new habits.

Writing daily in an anger journal is a third way to get to know your anger better and keep yourself accountable for working on soothing and restorative expression. In this journal you can not only express your anger to your heart's content, you can also keep track of anger triggers, incidents, questions, soothing techniques, and restorative-expression attempts. Over time, an anger journal can also become a remarkable record of healing and growth.

Finally, I encourage you to let the people closest to you know that you're struggling with anger and that you need their support. As you explore your anger and grow to better understand it, share your new insights with them. Openness and honesty will help you heal and them empathize. If any have been traumatized by your anger, they may not feel enough trust or engagement to actively support you, but it's still important for you to let them know that you're aware of your anger and are working on moving through and beyond it.

BEYOND ANGER

"Let us not look back in anger, nor forward in fear,
but around in awareness."
— James Thurber

Just as you will always feel grief over this loss, you may well continue to feel some anger. Anger can't be completely banished any more than grief can. After all, your anger is part of your grief! You wouldn't want to deaden yourself to anger, anyway. Anger is still a normal human emotion, and you shouldn't suppress your feelings or deny yourself the full range of emotional responses. But through intentional mourning, your healed anger and grief can become fully integrated parts of your life story.

So the goal moving forward isn't to be anger-free but instead anger-healthy. In addition to understanding, embracing, and restoratively expressing anger, here are some tools for living an anger-healthy life.

Have perspective and pick your battles
Before you choose to get worked up about something, ask

yourself: Will this still matter five years from now? If not, consider letting it go.

Practice presence and patience
Anger arises from unmet expectations. If you let the present moment unfold without expectations—and with patience when something frustrating does happen—you'll be slower to anger and faster to appreciation.

Forgive others and yourself
Forgiveness is a gift you give to yourself and others. It may not always be a gift you can offer, but when you can, you will find that, like all meaningful gifts given, it blesses you in return. Forgiveness often lifts a burden and replaces it with peace.

Cultivate a sense of humor
Sometimes when something unexpected happens, you can get mad, or you can laugh. The latter is often the way to go. A life filled with laughter or a life lived in anger? Choose wisely.

Lean on love
When you're angry, get in the habit of soothing yourself and then after you're calm, talking about it with someone who loves you.

Be grateful for grace

I think it might be impossible to feel deep gratitude and anger at the same time. When you can, focus on being grateful for the good instead of angry about the bad. Grace is receiving something good that you didn't earn or particularly deserve. When possible, allow yourself to lean into grace.

A FINAL WORD

"Holding onto anger is like grasping a hot coal with the intent of throwing it at someone else. You are the one who gets burned."
— Buddha

I again want to express my condolences. A grief marked by anger is often the result of an especially unfair loss. If this is the case for you, I am so sorry that it happened, and I am also sorry that you are among the unfortunate grievers forced to find your way through an especially challenging grief.

Regardless of the circumstances of your loss, your anger is justified and real. But so, too, is your responsibility to work on understanding, embracing, and restoratively expressing it. For yourself and for the people in your life, you have an obligation to move through and beyond your anger.

Life is precious and short. Beyond the early months or years of grief, every extra day spent in anger is a day you are not living and loving fully. I hope you will use this little book as a springboard to hope and healing. Godspeed.

Healing a Friend's Grieving Heart

When a friend suffers the loss of someone loved, you may not always know what to say. But you can do many helpful, loving things.

This book provides the fundamental principles of being a true companion, from committing to contact the friend regularly to being mindful of the anniversary of the death.

ISBN: 978-1-879651-265 • 128 pages • softcover • $11.95

Finding the Words

It's hard to talk to children and teens about death and dying, particularly when someone they love has died or might die soon.

This practical and compassionate handbook includes dozens of suggested phrases to use with children of all ages as you explain death in general or the death of someone loved. Also included are ideas and words to draw on when discussing death by suicide, homicide, or terminal illness.

ISBN: 978-1-61722-189-7 • 144 pages • softcover • $14.95

Grief One Day at a Time

After someone we love dies, each day can be a struggle. But each day, if we work to embrace our normal and necessary grief and care for ourselves, we will also take one step toward healing. Those who grieve will find comfort and understanding in this daily companion.

ISBN: 978-1-61722-238-2 • 384 pages • softcover • $14.95

All Dr. Wolfelt's publications can be ordered by mail from:
Companion Press, 3735 Broken Bow Road, Fort Collins, CO 80526
(970) 226-6050 • www.centerforloss.com

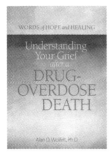

Understanding Your Grief After a Drug-Overdose Death

In this compassionate guide, Dr. Alan Wolfelt shares the most important lessons he has learned from loved ones who've picked up the pieces in the aftermath of a drug overdose. Readers will learn ideas for coping in the early days of their grief, as well as ways to transcend the stigma associated with overdose deaths. The book also explores common thoughts and feelings, the six needs of mourning, self-care essentials, finding hope, and more.

ISBN: 978-1-61722-285-6 • softcover • $9.95

Too Much Loss: Coping with Grief Overload

Grief overload is what you feel when you experience too many significant losses all at once, in a relatively short period of time, or cumulatively. Our minds and hearts have enough trouble coping with a single loss, so when the losses pile up, the grief often seems especially chaotic and defeating. The good news is that through intentional, active mourning, you can and will find your way back to hope and healing. This compassionate guide will show you how.

ISBN: 978-1-61722-287-0 • softcover • $9.95

All Dr. Wolfelt's publications can be ordered by mail from:
Companion Press, 3735 Broken Bow Road, Fort Collins, CO 80526
(970) 226-6050 • www.centerforloss.com

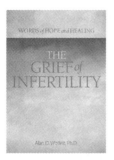

The Grief of Infertility

When you want to have a baby but are struggling with fertility challenges, it's normal to experience a range and mixture of ever-changing feelings. These feelings are a natural and necessary form of grief. Whether you continue to hope to give birth or you've stopped pursuing pregnancy, this compassionate guide will help you affirm and express your feelings about infertility.

By giving authentic attention to your grief, you will be helping yourself cope with your emotions as well as learn how to actively mourn and live fully and joyfully at the same time. This compassionate guide will show you how. Tips for both women and men are included.

ISBN: 978-1-61722-291-7 • softcover • $9.95

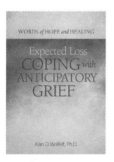

Expected Loss: Coping with Anticipatory Grief

We don't only experience grief after a loss—we often experience it before. If someone we love is seriously ill, or if we're concerned about upcoming hardships of any kind, we naturally begin to grieve right now. This process of anticipatory grief is normal, but it can also be confusing and painful. This compassionate guide will help you understand and befriend your grief as well as find effective ways to express it as you live your daily life.

ISBN: 978-1-61722-295-5 • softcover • $9.95

All Dr. Wolfelt's publications can be ordered by mail from:
Companion Press, 3735 Broken Bow Road, Fort Collins, CO 80526
(970) 226-6050 • www.centerforloss.com

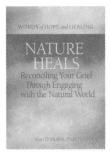

Nature Heals: Reconciling Your Grief Through Engaging with the Natural World

When we're grieving, we need relief from our pain. Today we often turn to technology for distraction when what we really need is the opposite: generous doses of nature. Studies show that time spent outdoors lowers blood pressure, eases depression and anxiety, bolsters the immune system, lessens stress, and even makes us more compassionate. This guide to the tonic of nature explores why engaging with the natural world is so effective at helping reconcile grief. It also offers suggestions for bringing short bursts of nature time (indoors and outdoors) into your everyday life as well as tips for actively mourning in nature. This book is your shortcut to hope and healing…the natural way.

ISBN: 978-1-61722-301-3 • softcover • $9.95

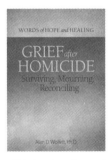

Grief After Homicide: Surviving, Mourning, Reconciling

Homicide creates a grief like no other. If someone you love died by homicide, your grief is naturally traumatic and complicated. Not only might your grief journey be intertwined with painful criminal justice proceedings, you may also struggle with understandably intense rage, regret, and despair. It's natural for homicide survivors to focus on the particular circumstances of the death as well. Whether your loved one's death was caused by murder or manslaughter, this compassionate guide will help you understand and cope with your difficult grief. It offers suggestions for reconciling yourself to the death on your own terms and finding healing ways for you and your family to mourn. After a homicide death, there is help for those left behind, and there is hope. This book will help see you through.

ISBN: 978-1-61722-303-7 • softcover • $9.95

All Dr. Wolfelt's publications can be ordered by mail from:
Companion Press, 3735 Broken Bow Road, Fort Collins, CO 80526
(970) 226-6050 • www.centerforloss.com

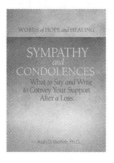

Sympathy and Condolences

When someone you care about has suffered the death of a loved one or another significant loss, you want to let them know you care. But it can be hard to know what to say to them or to write in a sympathy note. This handy book offers tips for how to talk or write to a grieving person to convey your genuine concern and support. What to say, what not to say, sympathy card etiquette, how to keep in touch, and more are covered in this concise guide written by one of the world's most beloved grief counselors. You'll turn to it again and again, not only after a death but during times of divorce or break-ups, serious illness, loss of a pet, job change or loss, traumatic life events, major life transitions that are both happy and sad, and more.

ISBN: 978-1-61722-305-1 • softcover • $9.95

The Guilt of Grief

Guilt and regret are two of the most common feelings in grief. The finality of death allows no more time for apologizing or making amends. There's no longer room for second chances. And so for many grievers it's normal to ponder "if-onlys" and experience the pain of mistakes made and opportunities squandered.

Yet shining the healing light of understanding and forgiveness on the guilt and regret of grief is within your power. If you befriend and find restorative ways to express these natural feelings, they will soften. This book offers the compassionate insight and tools you need to evolve from guilt to grace, one healing day at a time.

ISBN: 978-1-61722-315-0 • softcover • $9.95

All Dr. Wolfelt's publications can be ordered by mail from:
Companion Press, 3735 Broken Bow Road, Fort Collins, CO 80526
(970) 226-6050 • www.centerforloss.com

Complicated Grief

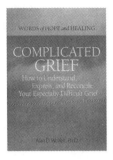

Grief is always difficult, but if yours feels especially painful, stuck, or complex, you may be experiencing complicated grief. Complicated grief is not an illness or disorder. It's simply normal grief that's been made more challenging by circumstances that overwhelm the person in mourning. If someone you love has died of suicide, homicide, or accidental causes; if the death was violent or premature or ambiguous; if you are struggling with additional life issues right now, such as health challenges (physical or mental), family problems, or financial stress; if your relationship with the person who died was extremely close or troubled; if you have suffered several losses in quick succession—this concise guide is for you.

In this compassionate resource by one of the world's most beloved grief counselors, you'll learn how complicated grief is different and what you can do to soften and eventually reconcile it. You'll inventory the reasons your grief is complicated. You'll learn the importance of engaging with and expressing your grief. And you'll find hope for your healing. There is a path through and beyond the wilderness of complicated grief. It's more arduous than most, but to live and love fully again, you must identify ways to walk this path that work for you. This book will show you the way.

ISBN: 978-1-61722-318-1 • softcover • $9.95

All Dr. Wolfelt's publications can be ordered by mail from:
Companion Press, 3735 Broken Bow Road, Fort Collins, CO 80526
(970) 226-6050 • www.centerforloss.com

ABOUT THE AUTHOR

Alan D. Wolfelt, Ph.D., is a respected author and educator on the topics of companioning others and healing in grief. He serves as Director of the Center for Loss and Life Transition and is on the faculty at the University of Colorado Medical

 School's Department of Family Medicine. Dr. Wolfelt has written many bestselling books on healing in grief, including *Understanding Your Grief, Healing Your Grieving Heart*, and *Grief One Day at a Time*. Visit www.centerforloss.com to learn more about grief and loss and to order Dr. Wolfelt's books.